The AI Edge: Unlocking Increased Productivity in Life and Work

AI in the Workplace

Adam Smith

Published by A. Smith Media, 2023.

THE AI EDGE: UNLOCKING INCREASED PRODUCTIVITY IN LIFE AND WORK

First edition. July 4, 2023.

ISBN: 979-8223965077

Written by Adam Smith.

Also by Adam Smith

AI in K-12 Education
Intelligent Machines in the Classroom: Unlocking the Potential of AI in K12 Education
Exploring the Possibilities: A Guide to Artificial Intelligence in K-12 Education
Exploring the Possibilities: AI in K12 Education
Making Sense of AI in K12 Education: A Guide for Teachers, Administrators, and Parents
The Future of Learning: Artificial Intelligence in K12 Education
Towards an AI-Infused Revolution in K12 Education
Unleashing AI in the Classroom: Strategies for Implementing Intelligent Technologies in K-12 Education
Unleashing the Potential of Artificial Intelligence in K-12 Education: Reimagining How Learning Happens
AI-Powered Learning: Advancing K12 Education for the 21st Century

AI in the Workplace
The AI Edge: Unlocking Increased Productivity in Life and Work

Breaking Down Bad Habits

Breaking Down Bad Habits: How to Overcome Self-Defeating Behaviors and Achieve Success

Standalone

Brain Dead: When It Comes To Improving Mental Health, What The Hell Are We Waiting For?

40 Things Intelligent People Do Daily

The Beginner's Guide to Quantum Computing & Mechanics

Open Source AI

Watch for more at https://books2read.com/adamsmith.

Table of Contents

Chapter 1: "Unlocking Increased Productivity with AI Automation: Optimizing Workplace Efficiency with Artificial Intelligence.................. 1

Chapter 2: "Maximizing Efficiency in the Workplace with AI Automation".. 3

Chapter 3: "Unlocking the Potential of AI: Harnessing Automation for Increased Efficiency and Productivity in the Workplace".................... 5

Chapter 4: "Unleashing the Benefits of AI: Streamlining Routine Work and Boosting Productivity" 7

Chapter 5: "Unlocking the Power of AI: Automating Routine Tasks and Enhancing Productivity in the Workplace".. 9

Chapter 6: "AI-Powered Automation: Leveraging Artificial Intelligence to Streamline Workplace Processes and Enhance Productivity.".. 11

Chapter 7: "The Benefits of AI Assistance for Enhancing Workplace Productivity".. 13

Chapter 8: "Harnessing the Power of AI to Streamline Workplace Tasks and Increase Productivity" 15

Chapter 9: "Harnessing AI to Unlock Productivity: Automating Routine Tasks in the Workplace"... 17

Chapter 10: "Harnessing the Power of AI to Streamline the Workplace and Unlock Productivity Gains"... 19

Chapter 11: "Unlocking the Potential of AI to Streamline Everyday Workplace Tasks and Increase Productivity." 21

Chapter 12: "Unlocking the Potential of AI: Enhancing Productivity Through Automation of Routine Tasks."........................... 23

Chapter 13: AI Introducing Automation and Improved Productivity in the Workplace.. 25

Chapter 14: "AI Automation to Improve Productivity: Unlocking the Power of Automation in the Workplace".. 27

Chapter 15: "Harnessing Artificial Intelligence for Maximum Work Efficiency: Automating Routine Tasks to Increase Productivity." 31

Chapter 16: "Leveraging AI to Streamline Workflows and Boost Productivity" 33
Chapter 17: "Maximizing Efficiency: Leveraging AI to Streamline Routine Tasks and Enhance Workplace Productivity" 35
Chapter 18: "Unlocking the Power of AI to Streamline Routine Workplace Tasks and Improve Productivity" 37
Chapter 19: "Unleashing the Power of AI: Automating Routine Tasks to Boost Productivity." 39
Chapter 20: "Harnessing the Power of AI: Automating Routine Tasks for Better Workplace Efficiency" 41
Chapter 21: "Unlocking the Power of AI: Automating Routine Tasks to Spark Productivity Gains" 43
Chapter 22: "Harnessing the Power of Artificial Intelligence to Streamline Business Processes and Boost Productivity." 45
Chapter 23: "Harnessing the Power of Artificial Intelligence to Modernize the Workplace and Increase Efficiency." 47
Chapter 24: "Unlock the Benefits of Artificial Intelligence: Streamlining Workplace Routine to Increase Productivity" 49
Chapter 25: "Unlock the Power of AI: Streamlining Everyday Work to Maximize Efficiency and Productivity." 51
Chapter 26: "Unlocking the Potential of AI: Automating Routine Tasks in the Workplace for Increased Productivity" 53
Chapter 27: "Unlocking the Potential of Artificial Intelligence in the Workplace: A Simple Guide to Automating Routine Tasks and Boosting Productivity" 55
Chapter 28: "Unlocking the Potential of AI: Automating Routine Office Tasks and Boosting Productivity." 57
Chapter 29: "Lighten Your Load: Harnessing the Power of AI Automation to Streamline Routine Tasks and Enhance Workplace Productivity." 59
Chapter 30: "Maximizing Efficiency Through AI Automation: Achieving Improved Productivity in the Workplace." 61

Chapter 1: "Unlocking Increased Productivity with AI Automation: Optimizing Workplace Efficiency with Artificial Intelligence.

Artificial Intelligence (AI) has revolutionized the idea of work processes and efficiency in the workplace. It can do more than reduce costs. This article will explore how companies can leverage AI automation to optimize workplace efficiency.

First, AI automation can enhance efficiency by helping to streamline repetitive and mundane manual tasks for employees. This is essential for freeing up time and resources for more critical charges and duties. With AI automation, many potential everyday tasks can be automated without compromising the outcomeThe writing is compelling and well-structured. However, one way to improve it would be to include real-life examples of how AI automation has been implemented in workplaces. This would provide readers with a better understanding of how AI automation can be beneficial for their own businesses. Additionally, including statistics or studies that show the positive impact of AI automation on workplace efficiency could further support the author's argument. These include tasks such as data entry, task scheduling, customer service, and research. By automating these processes, employees can focus on more valuable tasks and projects that help drive growth and success.

Secondly, AI automation provides organizations with valuable insights into process optimization. It can help collect and analyze data from operations in order to identify bottlenecks and potential areas for improvement. This can improve the employee experience by making operations smoother and faster. For example, AI-driven analytics can help identify inefficiencies in customer service processes, helping to improve customer satisfaction and loyalty. AI automation can also be used to identify potential areas of cost-cutting and improving efficiency.

Third, AI automation can help reduce the risk of human errors by helping to prevent mistakes caused by employee fatigue or distractions. This is especially important when dealing with complex processes such as financial accounting or the management of supply chains. AI automation can constantly monitor for potential errors and alert staff when discrepancies occur. This helps reduce the risk of costly mistakes and helps employees focus on tasks without worrying about potential errors.

Finally, AI automation can help create more insights into how teams interact within the workplace. It can help identify potential conflicts or communication problems between teams. AI automation can even provide insights on how to better organize teams and promote collaboration and cohesion.

AI automation is becoming more and more popular in businesses and can help unlock a great number of opportunities for increased productivity in the workplace. It can help automate mundane tasks, provide valuable insights on process optimization, reduce the risk of human errors, and improve team interactions. AI automation can be a powerful tool for unlocking a new level of efficiency and productivity in the workplace.

Chapter 2: "Maximizing Efficiency in the Workplace with AI Automation"

The use of artificial intelligence (AI) automation to enhance workplace efficiency is quickly becoming one of the most sought-after tools in the modern office. AI automation involves using computer programs, algorithms, or robots to streamline processes and maximize workforce productivity and cost efficiency. The use of AI has the potential to revolutionize the modern workplace, and many businesses are already capitalizing on its benefits.

The most obvious benefit of AI automation is its ability to save time on repetitive tasks. Using AI to automate certain processes can reduce the time and effort necessary for employees to complete mundane or repetitive tasks. AI can easily handle the same tasks that would otherwise require tedious manual labor, thus freeing up employee time and energy for more valuable project-driven work. Additionally, reducing the time spent filing or updating records gives employees more time and resources to focus on strategic projects, leading to increased operational efficiency and improved customer satisfaction.

AI automation can also reduce costs by improving efficiency and reducing the whole labor costs. AI algorithms can streamline processes, find patterns in data to highlight areas for improvement, and eliminate costly human errors resulting from an employee's lack of knowledge or a misread of a document. As robots become increasingly intelligent and capable of undertaking automated tasks, more of these things can be done automatically. This, in turn, reduces the number of employees necessary to complete the same task, while allowing those employees to focus on more beneficial initiatives.

AI automation tools can also make for better customer interactions. AI chatbots are becoming increasingly popular with businesses, as they provide intelligent and helpful customer service that can provide answers faster than a human can. By automating customer service inquiries and utilizing sophisticated AI algorithms, businesses can ensure that customers receive the help they need quickly and efficiently while freeing up their human employees to work on higher-priority tasks. Additionally, customer service bots can be created to provide more personalized customer service experiences, learn from customer interactions, and anticipate customer needs.

AI automation can also help to reduce workplace inefficiencies caused by the need for manual data entry or document storage, saving time and money. AI can easily automate tasks like data entry and document storage, reducing the need for employees to manually collect data or store records. Additionally, AI can be used to monitor and analyze data in real-time to identify areas of improvement or areas of potential errors, which can then be corrected quickly and efficiently.

AI automation can help to improve safety in the workplace. As robots become more capable and intelligent, they can be used to handle dangerous and repetitive tasks that would otherwise require human involvement. Automating these tasks allows for fewer employees in potentially hazardous scenarios while ensuring that safety protocols and regulations are followed to the letter.

AI automation can provide a plethora of benefits to businesses looking to maximize efficiency in the workplace. By automating mundane and time-consuming manual tasks, reducing labor costs, quickly providing customer service, automating data entry and document storage, and improving workplace safety, businesses can use AI automation to increase efficiency, reduce costs, and enhance customer satisfaction.

Chapter 3: "Unlocking the Potential of AI: Harnessing Automation for Increased Efficiency and Productivity in the Workplace"

In the modern world, technology is now an indispensable part of business operations. From basic office operations to complex analytics, Artificial Intelligence (AI) provides business owners with a smarter and more efficient way to operate their business and drive increased efficiency and productivity in the workplace.

The application of AI is often confused with automation, but automation is merely using machines to perform certain tasks instead of using human labor. In contrast, AI technology is designed to emulate human intelligence by combining complex algorithms and self-learning technologies with computers. AI can think, learn, and adapt to new trends, concepts, and tasks.

There are many potential applications of AI in the workplace, such as automated bots for customer service and virtual assistants for communicating with customers. AI can also automate repetitive tasks such as scheduling, data entry, and customer segmentation. Automation solves the problem of needing to find and hire skilled workers to complete tedious and often time-consuming tasks.

However, for business owners to truly unlock the potential of AI, they must strategically plan and strive to create an environment in which AI can play a successful role. To do this effectively, businesses should focus on implementing technology tools that are AI-friendly while considering the sort of data entry that is required and the type of output that is necessary.

Organizations also need to be careful not to become too enthralled by the potential of AI that they forget to consider how it will affect their employees. AI can benefit productivity and decision-making but can also create additional stress on employees or even lead to job cuts since machines are more efficient and cost-effective.

AI will need to be monitored and managed since it is constantly learning, meaning businesses will need the right talent and expertise to do this. AI systems will also need to be refined and adjusted on a regular basis in order to keep up with changing trends and to make sure it complies with all applicable laws and regulations.

As businesses continuously develop their AI capabilities, they will need to be mindful of the long-term implications of AI on both staff morale and customer satisfaction. AI is a powerful tool, but it is important to recognize and respond to any potential ethical concerns.

The continued interest of businesses look to take advantage of AI to increase efficiency and productivity in the workplace, they must have a clear roadmap in place to successfully implement AI technologies. With careful planning and considering the risks and benefits, organizations can benefit from increased efficiency and better decision-making. Ultimately, AI can be a powerful tool that can help unlock the potential of businesses in today's complex and competitive world.

Chapter 4: "Unleashing the Benefits of AI: Streamlining Routine Work and Boosting Productivity"

Artificial intelligence (AI) has revolutionized how businesses approach their operations and processes. AI technology can automate tedious and repetitive tasks, allowing businesses to streamline workflows and boost productivity. AI technology can also analyze large amounts of data, identify patterns, and provide insights for better decision-making. This can result in improved customer experience, greater efficiency, and cost savings. In this chapter, we will review some ways businesses are leveraging AI to streamline routine work and boost productivity.

The first way to utilize AI to streamline routine work is through automation. Through automation, robots are designed to do certain tasks, freeing up time for employees to focus on more important tasks. Automation can be used in a variety of different industries and can automate a wide range of activities from customer service to bookkeeping. Businesses that have embraced automation have reported improved customer service, increased efficiency, and have been able to free up valuable resources to focus on different projects.

The second way AI can streamline routine work is by utilizing data analysis. Data analysis is collecting and analyzing data to understand trends, behavior, and patterns. This can help businesses make better decisions and better understand the customer. AI can take the data and use algorithms to identify patterns and trends. This can lead to more meaningful insights, such as customer trends, product trends, and opportunities for improvement.

Another way AI can streamline routine work is through virtual assistants and chatbots. Virtual assistants are like personal assistants and can help with scheduling, responding to customer inquiries, and much more. Chatbots are computer programs that can answer customer inquiries or complete mundane tasks such as setting up appointments. Chatbots are becoming increasingly popular and can dramatically reduce the time it takes to respond to customer inquiries or execute routine tasks.

AI can also be used to streamline routine maintenance tasks. AI can be used to analyze data and identify potential problems. This can be extremely helpful in preventing downtime and further reducing costs. AI can also provide predictive maintenance solutions, allowing businesses to proactively address issues before they escalate and cause greater damage.

AI is becoming increasingly important in today's business world and can significantly benefit businesses. Through automation, data analysis, virtual assistants, and predictive maintenance, businesses can significantly reduce the time required for mundane, repetitive tasks. With AI technology, businesses can streamline their work processes and free up valuable resources to focus on more important tasks. AI technology can also provide insights into customer trends and behavior, providing businesses with a greater understanding of their customers and allowing them to make better, well-informed decisions. AI is enabling businesses to dramatically improve their operations and boost productivity.

Chapter 5: "Unlocking the Power of AI: Automating Routine Tasks and Enhancing Productivity in the Workplace"

AI, or artificial intelligence, has been transforming the workplace in recent years, creating new opportunities for companies to automate routine tasks and increase productivity. In order to fully realize its potential, however, businesses must understand how to unlock the power of AI in the workplace.

AI has revolutionized the way we work, giving us access to data and insights which can be used to shape and inform business decisions, allowing us to optimize employee performance and enhance customer service. AI-based automation technologies can streamline manual processes, such as inputting large amounts of data into a database, freeing up resources to focus on more creative activities, such as designing new products and services.

One of the biggest advantages of AI in the workplace is its ability to provide insights into customer behavior and preferences. With access to customer data, AI can not only help to identify opportunities for new products and services but can also help to improve the customer experience. For example, by understanding customer preferences, AI can tailor marketing campaigns to fit the needs of different groups of people or suggest relevant products and services that match user profiles.

Organizations can also use AI-powered analytics to identify patterns and spot trends in their datasets, helping to uncover opportunities for improvement. AI can detect anomalies in user behavior, identify the root cause of problems, and find the best way to solve them. This can provide valuable insights into optimizing processes and strategies, allowing organizations to stay one step ahead of the competition.

AI-powered automation can also help to free up time for employees by allowing them to focus on higher-level tasks, such as problem-solving and decision-making. Automation can also reduce the time it takes to process paperwork, saving time and costs associated with manual processes.

In order to unlock the full potential of AI in the workplace, organizations must take a strategic and proactive approach. AI technologies should be integrated into existing systems and processes rather than bolt-on solutions in order to maximize the benefits. It is also important to ensure that data is properly protected and managed, to ensure that customer privacy is upheld and the system's accuracy is maintained.

AI has the potential to revolutionize the way we work, freeing up resources and improving productivity. By understanding how to unlock the power of AI and integrating it into business processes and strategies, organizations can reap the rewards of improved decision-making and enhanced customer service.

Chapter 6: "AI-Powered Automation: Leveraging Artificial Intelligence to Streamline Workplace Processes and Enhance Productivity."

Integrating artificial intelligence (AI) into workplace processes has become an increasingly popular method of improving productivity and streamlining automation. AI-powered automation is a process that uses AI to automate business processes and tasks in an effort to maximize efficiency. AI-powered automation can automate manual tasks and reduce the need for employees to do repetitive and mundane tasks, freeing up their time to focus on higher-value activities.

AI-powered automation allows businesses to scale easily and become more efficient while improving employee productivity. AI-powered automation can automate a wide range of tasks, from data mining and customer service tasks to marketing and financial processing. It can also be used to automate routine tasks such as payroll and scheduling, as well as more complex areas like problem-solving and decision-making. AI-powered automation is becoming increasingly popular in warehouses, factories, and other manufacturing facilities, as it can improve processes and reduce the need for manual labor.

AI-powered automation can also be used to analyze data faster and more accurately than the human mind, which can then be used to save costs and create more efficient processes. AI-powered automation is particularly useful when it comes to predictive analytics and forecasting. By automating the predictive analytics process, businesses can predict market trends and other aspects of their operations faster and more accurately than ever before.

AI-powered automation also allows businesses to increase the speed of their operations and improve customer service. AI-driven chatbots can respond to customers' queries quickly and accurately, freeing up customer service personnel to focus on more important tasks. AI-driven virtual assistant systems can be used to automate mundane tasks such as scheduling meetings and ordering supplies, which can significantly reduce the amount of time and resources required to complete these tasks.

AI-powered automation can also be used to increase data accuracy and improve decision-making. AI-driven decision-making platforms can be used to automate decisions on topics such as pricing, segmentation, promotional campaigns, and customer segmentation. By automating these decisions, businesses can save time and improve accuracy by ensuring that decisions are based on accurate data.

The advantages of AI-powered automation are numerous, making it an attractive choice for businesses looking to streamline processes and improve employee productivity. AI-powered automation can automate mundane tasks, increase data accuracy, improve decision-making, and more. AI-powered automation can help businesses become more efficient and save on costs while ensuring employees can focus on higher-value activities. As a result, AI-powered automation can have a major positive impact on employee productivity and workplace operations.

Chapter 7: "The Benefits of AI Assistance for Enhancing Workplace Productivity"

The rise of artificial intelligence (AI) in the workplace has been revolutionary, bringing countless benefits to the working environment, from improved efficiency to heightened productivity. AI assistance is becoming increasingly common in an enterprise setting, with various AI tools and applications designed to make life easier for employees. In this chapter, we'll be looking at some key benefits of implementing AI assistance in the workplace and how they can help you to increase employee productivity.

AI assistance can provide unprecedented data analysis capabilities that can automate routine tasks. By collecting, researching, and analyzing data in an automated fashion, AI can enable businesses to gain valuable insights quickly and efficiently, making better decisions quicker than ever before. AI can provide its users with deep, thorough reports revealing hidden trends or patterns, allowing for better-informed business decisions. On the other hand, AI assistance can also act as a personal assistant for employees, providing help with their day-to-day tasks. AI can automate administrative tasks, saving employees time and allowing them to focus on more critical or creative tasks.

AI assistants can also help to streamline communication within organizations. AI can help manage emails, integrate different communication tools, and even serve as a virtual receptionist, assisting with customer service or other inquiries. This can mean fewer interruptions, greater efficiency, and less time spent on communication tasks.

AI assistance can help build smarter environments. AI technology in the workplace can automate repetitive tasks for employees and free them up to focus on more creative and imaginative projects. AI can automate routine parts of the workflow, such as accounting tasks or data entry. This can help workers to become more efficient as they can focus on activities that are more valuable to the company. AI can also be used to streamline HR processes, such as recruitment and onboarding, helping to increase productivity within the organization.

AI assistance can help to reduce human errors. Artificial intelligence algorithms are incredibly accurate and reliable, meaning they can free employees of the burden of making mistakes and provide them with accurate data, eliminating the risks of manual errors. AI can also help reduce security risks within the workplace. For instance, AI can be used to automatically detect and flag suspicious activity, helping to protect the organization from potential security threats.

There are numerous benefits to incorporating AI assistance at the workplace, from improved data analysis to smarter automation. AI can reduce manual errors and free up employees to focus on more productive tasks. Its ability to automate tasks, enhance communication, and provide insights can increase efficiency and ultimately lead to improved productivity in the workplace.

Chapter 8: "Harnessing the Power of AI to Streamline Workplace Tasks and Increase Productivity"

In recent years, Artificial Intelligence (AI) has become an integral part of modern business operations. From assistants that can automate processes and provide assistance in customer service to algorithmic decision-making tools that improve the accuracy of decisions taken within an organization, AI has become an indispensable tool for businesses of all sizes. In this article, we will be discussing the many ways AI can be used to streamline workflow tasks and increase workplace productivity.

At its core, AI is all about using sophisticated algorithms and data analysis to streamline tasks that typically require human intervention. This may include taking or personalizing customer orders, scheduling meetings, or optimizing user interfaces. By using AI to automate mundane tasks, organizations can focus more of their attention and resources on what really matters: their customers and their business strategy. With AI, businesses can quickly and easily complete essential tasks more efficiently, enabling them to get more out of the limited resources they have.

AI can also be used to provide tailored, real-time insights to businesses. By collecting and analyzing customer data, AI systems are able to generate tailored action plans and insights to guide decision-making. This helps maximize operational efficiency and identify areas where improvements may be needed. For example, AI-powered analytics can identify areas where customer demand is high, or where certain services are underutilized. By analyzing customer data, AI systems can generate tailored action plans to guide decision-making in real-time, ensuring organizations are able to better serve customers and maximize their profits.

AI can help improve workplace productivity by delivering personalized experiences to users. Through techniques such as natural language processing, AI systems can analyze customer data and deliver personalized content and services to customers. For instance, AI systems can analyze customer data and suggest the kinds of products and services that customers may be interested in. This helps to not only drive sales but also ensures that customers are more likely to return as a result of having a more positive experience with the company.

Harnessing the power of AI can help streamline workplace tasks and increase productivity in numerous ways. By automating mundane tasks, businesses can devote more of their resources to what really matters. Furthermore, AI can also be used to analyze customer data and deliver tailored insights and experiences, which can help drive sales and loyalty. In conclusion, there's no denying the power of AI to streamline workflow tasks and increase workplace productivity. By incorporating AI into the workplace, businesses of any size can make huge strides in efficiency, customer satisfaction, and profitability.

Chapter 9: "Harnessing AI to Unlock Productivity: Automating Routine Tasks in the Workplace"

In order to take full advantage of Artificial Intelligence (AI) as a tool to increase productivity in the workplace, it is vital to understand how to deploy it in the appropriate context and how to leverage it in order to unlock new possibilities and to create efficiencies in existing workflows. Increasingly, businesses are looking to AI automation to address the challenge of optimizing daily routines, allowing employees to focus on more value-adding activities.

When considering the range of tasks that are suitable for automation with AI, the primary focus should be on routine and often mundane, tasks that could be handled by machines faster and with greater accuracy. For example, in data entry and collection tasks, AI-driven systems can assist in automating the collection of required information. This may include collecting invoices, tracking delivery times and status, and monitoring and logging customer interactions. Additionally, automated tasks are suitable for mundane tasks such as email sorting and responding to customer inquiries, document and contract processing, and content curation.

The ability to automate tasks with AI also brings significant benefits to organizations in terms of cost savings. By automating mundane processes, businesses are able to reduce labor costs and free up time for human workers to focus on more critical tasks that require creativity, analytical thinking, and problem-solving. Additionally, with AI-driven automation, businesses are able to reduce the risk of human errors, as well as maximize efficiency by providing staff with access to real-time data and insights that may not otherwise be available.

In order to ensure that AI-driven automation is implemented successfully, it is essential to take a holistic approach that considers the organization's specific needs and objectives. To do this, businesses first need to identify the areas or tasks that can be automated using AI, and then define goals based on the desired outcome. Additionally, it is essential to ensure that the technology selected is suitable for the specific purpose in question and that it is tailored to the organization's culture. Finally, it can be beneficial to involve stakeholders from various departments to ensure that everyone is aware of the project's parameters and that the implementation is successful.

Ultimately, AI-driven automation can prove to be a very powerful tool to unlock greater productivity in the workplace by eliminating mundane tasks and reducing manual errors. By taking the time to invest in implementing the solution, businesses can achieve greater efficiency and freeing up resources to pursue more value-adding activities. Additionally, with AI driven automation, businesses can expect to experience cost savings, improved customer service, and access to real-time insights.

Chapter 10: "Harnessing the Power of AI to Streamline the Workplace and Unlock Productivity Gains"

In today's workplace, Artificial Intelligence (AI) is playing an increasingly important role in improving operations, enhancing customer experience, and providing dynamic insights. AI can provide numerous advantages to the workplace by automating the manual and time-consuming tasks, providing near-instant data insights, and improving customer service.

AI technology is proving to be a driving force in helping organizations to unlock productivity gains. AI is able to provide valuable insights into how companies can best streamline their operations. It can assess and analyze incoming data quickly, helping organizations to plan and prioritize tasks better. AI can provide business solutions for areas such as customer service and project management, eliminating the need for tedious and manual tasks, and freeing up personnel to focus on more productive tasks.

AI also offers organizations the opportunity to make better-informed decisions. Companies can utilize machine learning and AI algorithms to autonomously assess and analyze market trends and process data to help inform better decisions. Through predictive analytics, AI can also help to identify potential market trends and future customer behaviors, allowing organizations to better predict outcomes and plan ahead.

AI can also provide employees the opportunity to work smarter, not harder. AI can automate monotonous and complex tasks, as well as improve workflow and communication between systems. AI can alert employees of any issues that need their attention, so they can efficiently and quickly address them, enabling them to get back to higher-value tasks. AI can also be integrated into chatbots to provide employees with easy access to answers to their questions, saving time and allowing employees to be more productive.

AI technology is also playing a huge role in customer service. AI can help with customer service by providing more accurate recommendations and responses, and helping to provide a personal experience for each customer. AI-powered bots can provide quick responses and help customers find the answers and solutions they need faster.

By harnessing the power of AI, businesses can make vast improvements in the workplace. AI is capable of streamlining and automating manual and repetitive tasks, freeing up personnel to focus on more fulfilling and value-adding activities. AI is also helping to enhance customer service and provide dynamic insights, making it easier for organizations to anticipate customer behaviors and market trends. In addition, AI can provide opportunities for employees to work smarter, not harder, by providing them with the data they need to make informed decisions. By leveraging the power of AI, organizations are able to unlock immense productivity gains, and position themselves for future success.

Chapter 11: "Unlocking the Potential of AI to Streamline Everyday Workplace Tasks and Increase Productivity."

Artificial intelligence (AI) has created unprecedented opportunities for businesses to streamline everyday workplace tasks and increase productivity. AI has enabled businesses to automate mundane and time-consuming tasks such as document review, data entry, and customer service, allowing workers to focus their attention on more complex tasks that require deeper thought and problem-solving skills. AI can also be used to supplement or even replace traditional human staffing and lead to more efficient workflows and streamlined processes.

In its simplest definition, AI is a type of intelligent computer programming and logic that can be applied to everyday tasks and processes. AI systems are trained to understand and react to the environment they are in and make decisions accordingly. This technology uses automated algorithms and deep learning principles to identify patterns, trends, and relationships in data to solve problems and optimize tasks.

One of the most common uses of AI is natural language processing (NLP). This technology enables machines to understand the context and intent of human language and respond accordingly. For example, AI can be used to read employee emails or customer complaints and provide automated recommendations or actions. This saves employees the time and effort required to read all emails and customer feedback and then take action on them.

Another area where AI is being used to streamline everyday workplace tasks and increase productivity is in the processing of large volumes of information. AI can be used to quickly and accurately scan customer databases, sales records, and other data to identify trends and determine how best to take action. AI can also be used to automate the task of responding to customer inquiries. AI chatbots can be programmed to answer specific questions and provide helpful advice in a matter of seconds, eliminating the need for human resources to manually respond to customer inquiries.

AI can also be used to automate mundane tasks. AI can be used to trigger automated responses in a spreadsheet or a database when certain conditions are met. This can help employees answer routine questions without having to manually search for the answers. AI can also be used to schedule tasks and monitor performance so that businesses are continually improving and optimizing their processes.

AI can be used to increase productivity and reduce costs. AI can automate mundane and time-consuming tasks, freeing up human resources so that they can focus on more complex tasks. AI can also be used to streamline processes and increase efficiency, leading to cost and time savings.

The potential of AI to streamline everyday workplace tasks and increase productivity is clear. Businesses need to take advantage of this technology to stay competitive in today's business landscape and maximize their performance. AI's ability to automate mundane tasks and quickly process large amounts of data will help any organization remain agile and proactive in the face of changing business conditions.

Chapter 12: "Unlocking the Potential of AI: Enhancing Productivity Through Automation of Routine Tasks."

Technology has come a long way over the past several decades, opening up opportunities for businesses to improve productivity, accuracy, and efficiency. Artificial intelligence (AI) has quickly emerged as one of those technologies that are showing promise for automating certain routine tasks with greater accuracy and precision than ever before. In this chapter, we take a look at the potential of AI to enhance productivity through the automation of routine tasks.

To begin with, it is important to recognize the fact that AI is capable of performing certain tasks much faster and more accurately than any human worker. This can result in substantial gains in productivity as there are fewer mistakes that need to be corrected and fewer tasks that take longer before completion. AI is capable of analyzing data quickly and making recommendations or decisions with greater accuracy than humans due to its ability to assess and process large amounts of data in seconds. This is beneficial for businesses as it results in improved accuracy, faster decisions making processes, and, ultimately, higher productivity.

In addition to improved accuracy and faster decision-making processes, AI can also be used to automate certain mundane and tedious tasks. These tasks can range from data entry into an accounting system to scanning a document for specific keywords. As AI can quickly and accurately analyze data, it can automate these routine tasks more efficiently than traditional methods. This can help businesses save time and money, enabling them to focus resources on automating more complex tasks or processes. Automating such mundane and tedious tasks with the help of AI will open up more opportunities for businesses to maximize efficiency while minimizing costs.

AI can be used to streamline and improve the customer experience. AI-powered chatbots, for example can effectively engage with customers while helping them make better and more informed decisions. The ability to automate customer service processes with AI, while reducing human interaction and human intervention, can lead to greater customer satisfaction, improved customer loyalty, and, ultimately, higher profits.

AI can also be used to improve accuracy and productivity through automation of processes that involve manual labor. For example, robots and drones can be utilized for automated order picking, packaging, and sorting. This can be accompanied by machine vision to further enhance accuracy and productivity while reducing the need for manual labor. Over time, such automation of manual labor processes through AI-powered technologies can result in substantial time and cost savings for businesses.

As AI technology continues to evolve and become more advanced, businesses must recognize the potential it has to unlock new opportunities for enhanced productivity. While AI can automate certain routine tasks with greater accuracy and efficiency, businesses must plan their strategy and approach toward AI-driven automation carefully. Such careful planning can help businesses maximize the potential of AI while minimizing risks and ensuring that the needs of the customer are always met. Ultimately, as AI helps businesses automate more and more complex processes, it will become increasingly important for businesses to leverage AI technology to become more efficient and productive.

Chapter 13: AI Introducing Automation and Improved Productivity in the Workplace

AI introducing automation and improved productivity in the workplace is a widely debated issue in the modern business environment. Business owners are increasingly turning to AI to automate tasks, save time, and make their operations more efficient. On the one hand, AI presents an aspirational way to create efficiencies and improve productivity; on the other hand, it can be seen as a threat to the traditional methods of work, with the potential to automate jobs and ultimately replace people in the long term.

The introduction of AI to the workplace is an opportunity for increased efficiency and productivity. Automation, in particular, offers the major benefit of being able to complete repetitive, mundane tasks that would otherwise take humans' valuable time and mental effort, freeing them up to focus on higher-value tasks. AI can also help streamline operations, significantly reducing waste and improving production and delivery times for businesses. This can ultimately lead to increased productivity within the organization, helping them to remain competitive in their market while also increasing revenue.

However, there are also potential drawbacks to the introduction of AI and automation to the workplace. The most obvious is the risk of job loss, upskilling or retraining necessary for those whose roles are replaced by AI, and a decrease in wages due to increased competition from automation. Additionally, a lack of oversight in the use of AI presents the potential risk of malicious use, such as in the case of an AI-driven attack, or of automation gone wrong, resulting in financial losses. These potential risks need to be addressed and managed before businesses can move forward and successfully introduce AI into their operations.

Introducing AI into the workplace has the potential to improve productivity and create efficiencies. However, it is important to consider the potential risks and rewards of implementing AI to ensure that businesses make an informed decision and are able to successfully integrate automation into their operations. With careful management and consideration, businesses are well-positioned to take advantage of the benefits and productivity gains that AI can provide.

Chapter 14: "AI Automation to Improve Productivity: Unlocking the Power of Automation in the Workplace"

Artificial intelligence (AI) automation is a powerful tool that could help businesses increase their on the whole productivity. Since its introduction, AI automation has evolved from supporting a specific set of applications to managing entire processes in the workplace. Companies are starting to explore its use, in hopes of automating repetitive tasks and increasing efficiency in the workplace.

AI automation is the process of automating work tasks using algorithms and software that interpret and communicate commands at speed and accuracy. It captures data from sources such as user input and applies AI-driven algorithms to simultaneously analyze and understand them. AI automation promises to reduce manual labor and free up resources to focus on higher-value tasks.

AI automation can be used to automate mundane, repetitive tasks. It can also take over complicated tasks that require significant amounts of manual labor. This can ultimately lead to increased worker productivity and cost savings. For instance, customer service agents can process more requests due to automated responses. AI automated bots can take over data entry tasks and answer simple customer inquiries.

AI automation can also help reduce human error. For instance, humans can easily make mistakes while processing data. But AI automated software can process data and enforce rules quickly and accurately. AI-driven solutions can check for errors and accuracy, and notify the user in case of any potential mistakes. It can also detect anomalies and take corrective action to ensure that data is always accurate and up-to-date.

AI automation also enables businesses to generate accurate and timely insights. For instance, it can analyze large data sets and uncover hidden patterns and correlations. The data collected through AI automation can also be used to build more comprehensive models and predictions. This, related with other datasets, can enable businesses to make evidence-based decisions with confidence.

The implementation of AI automation will involve significant up-front costs, as well as ongoing investments in software and technology upgrades. Companies should carefully plan out the implementation of the technology to ensure a successful implementation. Cautious testing and optimization of the technology should also be included in any strategy for the implementation of AI automation.

Organizations must ensure that their employees are trained and upskilled to use AI automation tools. This may include creating training materials or enrolling employees in training sessions. Employees should also be given sufficient time to get accustomed to the technology and adjust to its use. It's also important to ensure that employees understand the benefits of using AI automation to increase productivity and optimize processes.

It's important to keep in mind that AI automation technology is not a "one size fits all" solution; it should be tailored to the needs of the organization. For example, some organizations may want to start by automating simple tasks and gradually increase the level of sophistication. Others may decide to implement more complex solutions right away. It's important to have the right mix of strategies to maximize the potential of AI automation and achieve maximum productivity.

AI automation is a powerful tool that can help businesses improve productivity by automating repetitive tasks and streamlining complex processes. But to ensure its successful implementation, businesses need to invest in requisite training and suitable tools that fit their needs. They should also monitor employee progress, apply continual optimization strategies, and continue to test new applications. With the right approach, businesses can maximize the potential of AI automation and unlock the power of automation in the workplace.

Chapter 15: "Harnessing Artificial Intelligence for Maximum Work Efficiency: Automating Routine Tasks to Increase Productivity."

A common struggle in the modern workplace is the challenge of productivity; it seems that despite our best efforts, it can be difficult to get as much accomplished in a day as we would like. Fortunately, advances in artificial intelligence (AI) have created a suite of technology that can be used to streamline the tasks associated with the average workday. Automating routine tasks is one of the most effective ways to use these technologies, as they have the potential to save valuable time and resources.

The use of AI in the workplace can be applied to virtually any job. Automation can be used in various areas, from data entry to customer service and more. In some situations, AI can even be used to provide insights that would otherwise be difficult or impossible to ascertain. This intelligence can be used to improve workflow processes and increase on the whole productivity.

For example, if you are running an online store, you can automate data entry procedures by integrating AI with the website's checkout process. This allows customers to quickly and easily complete a purchase. Additionally, AI can be used to provide customer service support, such as automated chatbots. They can be programmed to answer frequently asked questions and provide customer support, without requiring manual labor. This saves staff time while still providing customers with the help they need.

In a further case, businesses can use AI to streamline mundane tasks such as scheduling services. By using cloud-based AI platforms, businesses can tailor the scheduling process to fit their specific needs.

This can potentially save hours of manual labor and increase the whole efficiency of the organization.

AI can also be used to inform the decisions of management. By implementing AI-based analytics and decision-support tools, executives can quickly explore data and make more informed decisions. This saves time, eliminates manual labor, and allows executives to focus on their job — company strategy.

AI can also help organizations keep track of inventory and improve organizational efficiency. By leveraging AI, organizations can gain insight into inventory levels in real time. This allows them to make better decisions about what should be ordered and when. Additionally, they can also use AI to identify weak points in the inventory supply chain. All of this allows organizations to gain a better understanding of how their operations are working, leading to better planning and cost savings.

Overall, using AI in the workplace is a powerful tool for improving the workflow process and increasing productivity. It allows businesses to streamline tedious and mundane tasks and focus their energy and resources on more important tasks. It helps executives make informed decisions, leads to cost savings, and provides direct customer support. AI is quickly becoming an essential aspect of modern businesses and organizations, as it helps them gain a competitive advantage in today's ever-changing marketplace.

Chapter 16: "Leveraging AI to Streamline Workflows and Boost Productivity"

Artificial intelligence (AI) has been a game-changer in augmenting the productivity of businesses across the world. AI is being used in almost every vertical of the industry, to achieve greater efficiency and improved output. AI-enabled solutions are having a positive impact on businesses ranging from finance to retail. With its ability to automate certain tasks and analyze data with greater speed and accuracy, AI is allowing companies to take advantage of powerful analytics to enhance their workflow processes.

The first way companies can leverage AI to streamline workflows is by using AI-based software. AI-based software solutions are specifically designed to automate tedious processes that require a lot of manual data entry. For example, an AI-based software can be used to automate the entire process of data entry, from extracting relevant information from web forms to entering the data into a database. This type of automation can drastically reduce the time and effort required for manual data entry, thus boosting productivity.

Second, AI can also be used to automate the analysis of data. AI-enabled solutions allow businesses to acquire better insights into their data at a faster rate. This allows businesses to make better decisions in real time and optimize their processes for increased efficiency. For example, AI-based solutions allow retailers to identify the most popular trends in their industry, thus helping them adjust their stocks in real time.

Third, AI can also help with customer service. AI-enabled chatbots have become increasingly popular as a way to provide customers with 24/7 support. These chatbots can provide quick responses and help to customers based on predefined rules. They can also be smartly integrated into existing customer support teams, allowing companies to deliver better customer service while freeing up resources in their support staff.

Fourth, AI-enabled solutions can also be used to automate mundane tasks such as bookkeeping and accounting. These solutions can accurately handle a variety of calculations and financial statements, freeing up time and allowing businesses to focus on other important tasks. AI-based accounting and bookkeeping solutions are becoming increasingly popular and are drastically reducing the amount of time and effort required for bookkeeping and accounting tasks.

Lastly, companies can use AI-enabled solutions to automate decision-making. AI algorithms can make decisions faster and more accurately than humans, allowing businesses to make smart, data-driven decisions. For example, an AI-enabled system can be used to optimize pricing decisions for products, helping businesses maximize their profits and reduce losses.

Using AI to streamline workflows and boost productivity has become increasingly important for businesses of all sizes. AI is capable of automating mundane tasks, analyzing data faster and more accurately, providing customer support, and optimizing decision-making. With its ability to automate tedious processes and support businesses with data-driven analytics, AI is becoming an invaluable asset for businesses everywhere.

Chapter 17: "Maximizing Efficiency: Leveraging AI to Streamline Routine Tasks and Enhance Workplace Productivity"

Modern technology has revolutionized the way that companies around the world operate. In particular, advances in artificial intelligence (AI) have had a significant impact on how businesses handle their routine tasks and increase their workplace productivity. AI-enabled automation has been successful in streamlining processes, improving efficiency, reducing costs, and increasing on the whole throughput. As a result, more and more corporations are turning to AI to gain a competitive edge.

At the core of it, AI can be used to automate and streamline routine tasks that are typically performed manually. This provides an advantage in terms of time, labor, and accuracy—all of which translate into cost savings and increased efficiency. Some of the ways that businesses can use AI to maximize efficiency include:

Automated Scheduling: AI can be used to automate mundane scheduling tasks such as allocating resources, creating workflows, and generating reports. This helps to improve the accuracy of the scheduling and maximizes employee productivity, as employees can focus on more value-added tasks.

Predictive Maintenance: AI can be used to detect and identify potential issues before they arise. By analyzing patterns and trends, AI can help define what action to take in order to effectively address issues before they become major problems. This helps to reduce maintenance costs and increase uptime for production processes.

Data Analytics: AI-driven analytics can be used to identify trends and patterns in data in order to reveal potential areas of improvement. This helps organizations to quickly identify issues and take corrective action, in order to increase their efficiency.

Analyzing Human Behavior: AI-enabled analytics can be used to analyze employee behavior and to identify areas of improvement. AI can be used to recognize patterns in employee performance and to suggest the steps to take in order to maximize efficiency.

Customer Service: AI can also be used to automate customer service processes, helping to increase speed and accuracy. AI bots can provide automated customer service 24/7, without the need to hire additional personnel.

These are only a few of the ways that businesses can use AI to streamline routine tasks and increase their work efficiency. In today's competitive business environment, maximizing efficiency and increasing productivity are essential for survivability. AI-driven automation is playing a major role in helping organizations stay competitive and gain an edge over the competition. By leveraging the power of AI, businesses can streamline routine tasks, reduce costs, increase throughput, and ultimately gain a competitive advantage.

Chapter 18: "Unlocking the Power of AI to Streamline Routine Workplace Tasks and Improve Productivity"

Using Artificial Intelligence (AI) technology to automate routine tasks in the workplace has become a significant trend in recent years, as businesses realize the untapped potential for optimizing processes, increasing productivity and reducing costs. AI promises to revolutionize many aspects of the workplace, from digital assistants that streamline workflow and automate communication, to advanced analytics systems that uncover hidden patterns in data and provide actionable insights. The potential of AI to improve workplace productivity is immense, but it is only recently that we have had the technology and tools to unlock this potential.

In order to maximize the benefits that AI can offer, companies need to understand how to channel its power and use it to automate the most repetitive and routine tasks. AI can be used to automate mundane and time-consuming tasks, such as data entry and filing, freeing up employees to focus on more important projects. AI-driven automation can also speed up the process of searching through large volumes of data to find specific pieces of information. This reduces the time spent manually combing through records and allows employees to spend more time on high-value activities.

AI can also help to streamline decision-making processes. Predictive analytics algorithms can take inputs from past performance and suggest the best course of action, based on the insights gleaned from the data. By providing actionable recommendations in real time these algorithms can free up employees to focus on more important tasks while still improving efficiency.

An essential part of maximizing the potential of AI is making sure that it is integrated seamlessly into existing workflows. To achieve this, companies need to ensure that they have an AI infrastructure in place. This can include integrating existing software systems with AI-driven solutions, making sure all data is properly labeled and organized, and creating an open and collaborative environment for ongoing development.

AI can also be used to improve communication between different departments and teams within the workplace. Chatbots can answer commonly asked questions, schedule meetings, track progress, and even take input from employees to generate new ideas. By empowering employees to ask questions, provide feedback, and collaborate more easily, chatbots can help to improve workplace satisfaction and boost productivity.

AI can dramatically improve customer service. Chatbots can instantly answer customer queries, analyze customer behavior and even predict customer needs. This makes it easier for companies to quickly identify customer problems and customize solutions to meet their individual needs. In addition, AI can be used to automate marketing campaigns and sales processes, ensuring that customers receive the best possible experience.

AI technology has the potential to revolutionize the workplace. By automating mundane tasks, improving communication, and optimizing customer engagement, AI can have a dramatic impact on efficiency and productivity. Companies just need to ensure that they take the necessary steps to set up an agile AI infrastructure and integrate it into their existing processes. From there, they can take advantage of the substantial benefits that AI has to offer.

Chapter 19: "Unleashing the Power of AI: Automating Routine Tasks to Boost Productivity."

The potential of artificial intelligence (AI) to revolutionize the way we do business is one of the most talked-about buzzwords of the current era. AI can revolutionize how we do business, drive growth, and optimize everyday operations. From harnessing machine learning capabilities to automating routine tasks, AI is set to become the go-to tool for long-term success and efficiency. In this chapter, we'll look at how to use AI to automate routine tasks to boost productivity and efficiency.

AI is a technology that combines various components, including algorithms, data, inference, and visualizations, to perform intricate tasks the same way humans would, except faster and more accurately than ever before. Machine learning technology allows AI to make predictions, find correlations and recognize patterns in data that humans would typically have to sift through manually. This is why AI is invaluable for a range of tasks and businesses that have formerly been time-consuming and labor-intensive.

One example of a task where AI can particularly excel and improve efficiency is data management. AI-powered algorithms automate the tedious task of manually entering, sorting, and analyzing data. AI can also enable a more streamlined and comprehensive view of customer databases, market segmentation, and insights. This level of organization and analysis simplifies and speeds up data-driven decision-making processes while allowing businesses to save time and money.

Aside from data management, AI can assist businesses in their customer service operations. Intelligent chatbots powered by AI can help customers quickly resolve problems and answer questions without having to deal with a human customer service representative. By automating the customer service process, businesses can focus on more important tasks, such as refining the customer journey and providing on-demand services and solutions. AI-powered voice assistants such as Alexa and Siri have already been used to great success in the customer service and retail sectors.

AI can also be used to automate scheduling, workforce management, and payroll processes. By leveraging AI technology to handle employee and job scheduling, businesses can create searchable databases and track workforce performance in order to better allocate resources and tasks. By automating this process, businesses can save valuable time and resources while keeping everyone on top of their tasks.

AI technology can help businesses automate their marketing tasks, such as sending emails, optimizing campaigns, and personalizing customer experiences. Email marketing campaigns are often the most effective form of digital marketing, and AI-powered tools can automate the creation, scheduling, and sending of email campaigns. AI-powered technologies can also automate the segmentation process, allowing businesses to design marketing campaigns based on customer preferences and buying patterns. It can also be used to automate tasks such as sorting customer service emails according to urgency and responding appropriately.

When implemented correctly, AI can be a powerful tool for businesses to unlock efficiency and drive productivity. AI technology can automate a range of tedious and labor-intensive tasks, such as data management, customer service, scheduling, and marketing. By doing so, businesses can capitalize on the power of AI and create a streamlined and automated workflow that improves efficiency and saves time and money. Leveraging the power of AI is an essential step in today's business landscape and an effective way to drive long-term success.

Chapter 20: "Harnessing the Power of AI: Automating Routine Tasks for Better Workplace Efficiency"

In recent years, artificial intelligence (AI) has been revolutionizing how businesses operate and has enabled greater automation of routine tasks, resulting in improved workplace efficiency. More and more companies are now taking advantage of the potential of AI to reduce costs, speed up processes, and improve customer service. The potential benefits of AI are immense, but harnessing the power of AI requires careful consideration and planning.

AI is essentially about using data and algorithms to make decisions. By leveraging AI-enabled tools such as machine learning, natural language processing, and computer vision, companies can automate tedious and time-consuming tasks. This automation can save time and money, as well as improve accuracy since it eliminates the possibility of human error. AI-driven automation also decreases the workload for employees, freeing up their time to focus on higher-value tasks and eliminating the need for manual intervention.

Organizations are also able to leverage AI for better efficiency in customer service processes. By creating customer service chatbots that use natural language processing (NLP) to interact with customers, companies can reduce customer wait times and increase customer satisfaction. These bots can handle routine inquiries, freeing up company resources to handle more complex issues. AI-driven customer service chatbots also reduce customer wait times by providing instant responses to customer inquiries and handling multiple customer requests simultaneously.

AI can also be used to improve employee engagement and productivity. AI-enabled tools such as gamification and virtual assistants can increase employee engagement by providing motivational challenges and suggestions tailored to individual needs, allowing employees to better meet their goals. AI-driven analytics tools can also be used to analyze employee data, helping to identify areas of improvement and providing valuable insights into employee performance.

AI can help organizations improve process efficiency by reducing lead time and increasing turnaround speed on tasks. AI-driven automation can reduce the amount of time spent on manual tasks, such as data entry and document scanning. By using AI to automate mundane tasks, organizations can free up resources to focus on more complex and high-value tasks. Furthermore, AI-driven automation can also help reduce labor costs and reduce the need for costly human labor.

Harnessing the power of AI can help organizations achieve significant workplace efficiency improvements. AI-enabled automation can reduce the time spent on mundane and routine tasks, allowing employees to focus on more complex and higher-value tasks. Additionally, AI can improve customer service processes and increase employee engagement and productivity. By leveraging AI-driven tools, organizations can reduce costs, improve customer satisfaction, and on the whole, create a better working environment.

Chapter 21: "Unlocking the Power of AI: Automating Routine Tasks to Spark Productivity Gains"

In recent years, Artificial Intelligence (AI) has been finding its way into our daily lives, from chatbot customer service agents to automated voice assistants. AI has the potential to revolutionize industries by unlocking its power to automate routine tasks and spark productivity gains. Companies from different sectors, including banking, healthcare, and retail, have already started taking advantage of AI technologies to improve operational efficiency and customer experience.

At its core, AI is a multifaceted approach to problem-solving that includes machine learning, natural language processing, and robotic process automation. By leveraging AI, businesses have the opportunity to automate time-consuming and mundane tasks such as data entry and manual processes, freeing up resources that can be used to focus on more complex and creative projects.

Machine learning (ML) is a form of AI that allows computer applications to learn and adapt from experience. Using data from previous experiences, ML algorithms enable computers to learn and conduct operations without requiring explicit instructions. Banks now use ML to automate the process of approving credit applications and analyzing customer behavior.

Meanwhile, natural language processing (NLP) is AI technology that enables computers to understand human language. This technology has been used within customer support to automate customer service tasks, and within healthcare to power virtual health assistants. NLP also allows AI chatbots to respond to questions and queries from customers naturally.

Finally, robotic process automation (RPA) is a form of AI designed to automate complex, repeatable tasks without the need for human intervention. RPA can be used to generate massive productivity gains by reducing the number of manual processes and repetitive tasks that need to be completed. RPA is already being used by organizations within the legal, accounting, and financial services sectors to save costs and free up resources.

Unlocking the power of AI offers companies the opportunity to boost productivity, reduce costs, and improve customer experience. For example, AI-powered chatbots enable businesses to provide faster customer service by automatically answering queries and taking over mundane tasks such as data entry. And NLP is being used to analyze customer feedback and assist with product recommendations.

AI is an invaluable tool for organizations looking to gain competitive advantages in today's digital world. By automating redundant, mundane tasks, AI has the power to unlock productivity gains, increase operational efficiency, and improve customer experience. With these opportunities in mind, it's clear that AI will continue to be a major factor in the success of organizations in the years to come.

Chapter 22: "Harnessing the Power of Artificial Intelligence to Streamline Business Processes and Boost Productivity."

In recent years, Artificial Intelligence (AI) has become a popular new way to streamline workflows, automate mundane tasks, and improve efficiency. It can be used to supplement human capabilities, allowing companies to more easily remain competitive and productive. This article will explore the various ways that AI can be used to harness the power of the business process, boost productivity, and improve customer service.

First, AI has the potential to improve customer service by automating repetitive tasks and providing more accurate and immediate responses. For example, customer service agents no longer have to manually review customer queries and answer common questions. AI systems can quickly answer questions with 24x7 customer service, freeing up time for more important tasks. AI can also be used to monitor customer conversations and provide real-time recommendations based on customer need. This allows for faster and more accurate responses, leading to better customer experiences.

Second, AI can be used to speed up production and manufacturing processes. Automation and machine learning can be used to optimize task orders, improve the accuracy of forecasts, reduce workforce fatigue, and scale production levels. AI-powered robots can eliminate labor costs by performing tasks that used to require manual labor. This increases manufacturing efficiency and can drastically reduce costs, resulting in more productive and profitable businesses.

Third, AI-powered analytics are also a great way to monitor performance and yield data-driven insights. By analyzing large datasets, AI can detect patterns and search for abnormalities. This helps identify operational problems and close gaps in processes. AI helps to improve efficiency, accuracy, and consistency, which can translate to better customer service and increased output.

Fourth, AI can be used to support decision-making in the workplace. This can lead to improved outcomes by providing insights into better ways of executing business strategies. AI algorithms can help managers predict customer behavior, identify performance problems, and validate data accuracy. Using analytics tools to detect problems at early stages can also help manage risks and reduce undesirable outcomes.

Fifth, AI is also great for optimizing the workplace environment. AI-powered bots can keep track of employee engagement and help automate mundane HR tasks, speeding up the recruitment process and increasing on the whole efficiency. Smart machines and robots can also aid companies in reducing labor costs, as they can help increase process productivity and accuracy without the need for additional personnel.

Finally, AI is a powerful tool for predicting future trends and helping organizations stay ahead of the competition. Companies can use predictive analytics to accurately forecast customer demand, which helps provide better insights into future marketing and product development. AI-powered bots can also be used to conduct data mining and uncover new data trends, which can then be used to come up with better products and services.

The use of AI in business processes and workplace operations can improve productivity and efficiency in a variety of ways. AI can be used to automate mundane tasks, monitor customer conversations, streamline production, and gain data-driven insights from analytics. It will also help reduce costs, support decision-making, and optimize workplace conditions. AI is an essential technology that should form a key part of any modern business's operation.

Chapter 23: "Harnessing the Power of Artificial Intelligence to Modernize the Workplace and Increase Efficiency."

Artificial intelligence (AI) has the potential to revolutionize the modern workplace and increase efficiency by automating many of the mundane, labor-intensive tasks that slow down productivity and add cost. The use of AI-driven automation can help reduce the time it takes to perform specific tasks, freeing up employees to focus on higher-value activities and fostering collaboration. With suitable investments in AI technology, organizations can create an intelligent, efficient, and more competitive workplace.

At the heart of AI technology are intelligent algorithms. Machine learning, natural language processing (NLP), and deep learning are all subsets of AI technology that can be applied to help organizations achieve efficiency gains. Machine learning refers to the ability of a computer system to learn without being explicitly programmed. NLP is the ability of a computer to recognize and understand language. Deep learning is a type of machine learning that uses layered deep neural networks to identify complex patterns in data.

Organizations interested in leveraging AI's power to modernize their workplaces should begin by assessing their needs. The key is to determine how AI automation can be used to improve efficiency and productivity, reduce labor costs, and achieve optimal resource utilization. Once the needs have been identified, organizations can select the appropriate AI technology that best fits their needs.

AI can be used in a variety of ways to modernize the workplace. Chatbots and intelligent virtual assistants can be used to automate customer service inquiries and mundane business tasks. AI-enabled document processing algorithms can read, understand, and interpret documents quickly and accurately. AI-assisted project management agents can monitor employee and contractor performance and provide feedback and guidance. Digital assistants can be used to generate automatic reports and presentations, freeing up time for other tasks.

Modern organizations recognize AI's potential to increase efficiency and help them stay competitive. AI-enabled automation has helped streamline processes, reduce labor costs, and increase productivity, making companies more competitive in both domestic and global markets. Companies like Microsoft, Google, and Amazon use AI to automate mundane tasks such as data entry, customer inquiries, and document generation, freeing employees to focus on higher-value activities.

The use of AI-enabled automation has also helped create an intelligent, efficient, and competitive workforce. AI-driven tools such as intelligent virtual assistants and chatbots are assisting companies to provide better customer service and enhance employee collaboration. AI-enabled project management agents offer feedback and guidance to employees and contractors, helping them do their jobs faster. Organizations that are leveraging AI are realizing increased efficiency and productivity, as well as greater return on investment.

AI will continue to play a critical role in the modern workplace as organizations seek to stay competitive in the future of work. AI-enabled automation can help organizations increase efficiency and productivity while reducing labor costs. Suitable investments in AI technology and the correct use of AI in the workplace can go a long way toward transforming the future of work and helping businesses stay competitive.

Chapter 24: "Unlock the Benefits of Artificial Intelligence: Streamlining Workplace Routine to Increase Productivity"

In today's world, the integration of technology into the workplace is more important than ever before. The use of artificial intelligence (AI) is one of the most significant ways in which companies can leverage technology to improve workplace efficiency and productivity. AI has the potential to not only reduce the amount of time it takes to complete repetitive tasks, but it can also unlock the potential of data, analytics, and insight to boost innovation, customer service, and on the whole business performance.

AI has already become an essential tool for streamlining workplace processes in a wide range of industries. In manufacturing, for example, AI can be used to automate production processes, reduce production delays, and increase quality control. In retail, AI can be used to improve customer service and reduce the amount of time required to fulfill orders. In healthcare, AI can be used to quickly and accurately diagnose illnesses and diseases, allowing for improved patient outcomes.

AI has also been used to streamline the recruitment process, allowing companies to quickly and accurately assess potential candidates with predictive analytics. This helps to ensure that the most qualified candidates are selected to fill available job openings. AI can also streamline workplace communication by automatically sequencing emails and sorting messages, ensuring that critical information is efficiently and quickly delivered.

AI has the ability to greatly reduce the amount of time required to complete frequent and mundane administrative tasks. AI can be used to quickly create charts, diagrams, and other types of visual information from data sets. This can be used to automatically generate reports and dashboards, allowing for more efficient analysis and decision-making.

AI also has the potential for automating manual tasks such as payroll processing and invoicing, freeing up more time for other activities such as innovation and idea generation.

Getting the most out of AI in the workplace will require an effective deployment of the technology. This means that companies must invest in the right infrastructure, support personnel, and data sets to ensure that AI technologies can be used to their full potential. Additionally, there must be a strong commitment to using the data from these technologies to inform and impact decision-making and strategy.

The use of AI has the potential to significantly increase workplace productivity and efficiency. By streamlining routine tasks, organizations can free up time and resources for more important activities such as research and development and customer service. AI can also provide valuable insights into industry trends, allowing companies to make more informed decisions and stay ahead of the competition. If implemented correctly, AI can be the key to unlocking a range of business opportunities that will help organizations thrive.

Chapter 25: "Unlock the Power of AI: Streamlining Everyday Work to Maximize Efficiency and Productivity."

The rise of artificial intelligence (AI) over the past decade has revolutionized the way we work. AI has enabled us to automate routine tasks, streamline processes, and maximize efficiency and productivity. As AI technology continues to evolve and become more sophisticated, AI applications can be found in almost every industry, from healthcare to food technology. While AI can be seen as a major disruptor of traditional workflows, it can also be leveraged to create powerful new solutions that can unlock the potential of existing and emerging technologies.

In order to successfully implement AI into everyday work, organizations must first understand how AI can be used to maximize efficiency and productivity. AI's ability to process large volumes of data quickly and accurately makes it a powerful tool in streamlining workflows. AI can be used to automate mundane tasks, such as document or data entry, that can be time-consuming and tedious. Automation can help to greatly simplify processes, reduce errors, and free up personnel to focus on more value-added tasks.

AI can also be used to provide a more accurate analysis of data. In healthcare, AI-powered bots are capable of quickly and accurately analyzing vast amounts of data and monitoring patients. This can help to identify patterns and give medical professionals a better understanding of a patient's health and provide more accurate treatment recommendations. Similarly, AI can be used to analyze large amounts of financial data, which can help investments teams spot trends, identify areas of improvement, and make more informed decisions.

Another powerful use of AI is its ability to support intelligent decision-making. Organizations can use AI to identify areas for improvement and develop customized workflows based on specific business needs. Advanced Machine Learning algorithms can be used to optimize processes and improve the accuracy of predictions. AI can also be used to help with customer service inquiries and automate transactions in order to reduce costs and improve efficiency.

AI can also be used to increase efficiency and productivity by driving innovation. AI-driven research and development initiatives can uncover new possibilities in existing products and services or in totally new directions. AI can unlock the potential of emerging technologies and give organizations the competitive edge they need to stay ahead of the curve in a rapidly changing world.

In order to truly maximize the potential of AI, organizations must also consider how they will manage and control the technology. AI governance is the key to unlocking AI's full potential. Governance is needed to ensure that AI is deployed safely and ethically and that it is used in a manner that is in line with the organization's values and objectives. Ensuring that the data being used is accurate and secure can help maximize the effectiveness of AI-driven technologies.

The rise of AI has enabled us to unlock new possibilities in streamlining everyday work and maximizing efficiency and productivity. By leveraging AI to automate mundane tasks, provide more accurate analysis of data, improve decision-making, and drive innovation, organizations can unlock the power of this rapidly evolving technology. Implementing proper AI governance procedures and ensuring data accuracy and security are also key to ensuring effective AI deployment.

Chapter 26: "Unlocking the Potential of AI: Automating Routine Tasks in the Workplace for Increased Productivity"

The potential for automation to revolutionize the workplace lies at the heart of the possibilities offered by Artificial Intelligence (AI). Automation entails the application of technology to streamline the decision-making process and optimize efficiency across repetitive tasks, reducing human error and freeing up workers for roles requiring more strategic thinking and creative problem-solving. As AI technology continues to evolve, it is increasingly being adopted by organizations in various industries to transform their practices and improve employee productivity.

At its core, automation focuses on leveraging repetitive processes and tasks to enhance efficiency, accuracy, and speed. AI can be utilized to automate mundane, time-consuming tasks, such as data-entry and interfacing with customers or vendors. Robotic Process Automation (RPA) is a type of technology that is used to streamline and automate manual processes, such as budget tracking or report generation. It is also capable of automating IT processes such as software engineering, programming, and system maintenance. RPA has been successfully deployed to address customer service demands in several industries, including retail, banking, healthcare, and insurance.

As AI becomes more developed and accessible, automation will further revolutionize the workplace and provide organizations of all sizes the opportunity to capitalize on efficiency, accuracy, and cost savings. Automation will be used to increase the speed of knowledge transfer and generate more accurate predictions. By eliminating manual tasks and optimizing decision-making processes, AI can render useful insights into customer preferences and behavior. Companies can then utilize this data to inform their product designs and tailor their services to meet the changing preferences of their target consumer base.

AI has the potential to make profound changes in the workplace, such as simplifying and automating ordering systems, communication tools, scheduling tools, time tracking, and productivity tracking. This technology can also be deployed more broadly to replace low-income jobs such as those in the service industry. AI-driven automation has the potential to reduce labor costs and free up employees for roles requiring more skill and creativity.

The use of automation in the workplace is not without its challenges. AI is still a relatively new technology, and its capabilities are being rapidly developed and updated. This uncertainty can create challenges for organizations in terms of successfully deploying the technology and addressing implementation issues. Furthermore, the need to continuously update AI technology to keep up with the fast-changing technological landscape can result in significant costs for companies.

AI can automate routine tasks in the workplace, resulting in increased productivity and cost savings. AI-backed automation can optimize decision-making processes and increase the speed of knowledge transfer. Moreover, organizations can use this technology to better serve their customers and tailor their services to meet changing preferences. The potential of automation is only just beginning to be realized; with continued development and investment, AI's capabilities will continue to expand, transforming the workplace and improving efficiency.

Chapter 27: "Unlocking the Potential of Artificial Intelligence in the Workplace: A Simple Guide to Automating Routine Tasks and Boosting Productivity"

In recent years, the use of Artificial Intelligence (AI) in the workplace has become increasingly popular, as businesses have begun to leverage its power to automate routine tasks and improve efficiency. By leveraging AI technologies, businesses have been able to free up valuable human resources and reduce labor costs while boosting their on the whole productivity. In this chapter, we will discuss how businesses can unlock the potential of AI in the workplace by leveraging its capabilities to automate routine tasks and improve on the whole efficiency.

To begin, businesses must first understand the potential that AI technology offers. AI technologies are capable of autonomously performing a variety of tasks, such as data analysis, customer service, production, and more. Employing AI technologies can reduce the amount of labor that is required to perform complex tasks, allowing employees to focus more on creative problem-solving and growth opportunities. Additionally, AI technologies offer a variety of advantages, such as increased accuracy, improved scalability, and other features that can enhance the efficiency of a business.

Once businesses have a basic understanding of the potential of AI in the workplace, they must then consider how to best leverage its capabilities. For example, businesses can use AI technologies to automate routine tasks that are time-consuming and require repetitive actions. Additionally, AI technologies can be used to identify potential issues and opportunities in the workplace, allowing them to be addressed quickly and efficiently. Finally, businesses can leverage AI to help identify potential customer service issues before they arise, allowing them to provide a better on the whole experience to their customers.

In order to successfully use AI to improve efficiency in the workplace, businesses must first ensure that the systems are properly integrated and configured. Additionally, businesses should ensure that their staff is familiar with how to operate and monitor AI systems, in order to maximize its effectiveness and make sure that any potential issues are identified and addressed immediately. Besides, organizations must ensure that the data being used is being gathered properly, processed correctly, and analyzed accurately for optimal use. By ensuring that these conditions are met, businesses can ensure that their AI system is providing the most value and helping promote a productive and successful workplace.

Finally, businesses should explore how AI can be leveraged to create new products and services that can help them remain competitive in the marketplace. AI technologies can be used to create new products and services that are tailored to a business's specific needs, allowing them to remain competitive and address customer needs quickly and efficiently. Additionally, AI technologies can also be used to design process and workflow improvements that can result in increased efficiency and cost savings.

By understanding how to unlock the potential of AI in the workplace, businesses can effectively use AI technologies to automate tasks, improve customer service, and create new products and services. By leveraging AI's potential, businesses can gain the competitive edge in the marketplace and achieve new heights of success.

Chapter 28: "Unlocking the Potential of AI: Automating Routine Office Tasks and Boosting Productivity."

In today's world, Artificial Intelligence (AI) has become a hot topic, and businesses are starting to realize the potential of using AI to automate routine office tasks, thus boosting productivity. It is possible for businesses to tap into this new technology to unlock broader and more profound applications to their organization.

Today's AI technology has been developed with the goal of automating routine office tasks. This eliminates time-consuming manual work and leverages the power of technology to supercharge a business's performance. AI can transform mundane tasks such as data entry, report generation, and email sorting into more efficient processes. Furthermore, businesses can utilize AI to provide predictive data analysis, thus providing better insights into customer needs and empowering better decision-making.

Another way AI can assist businesses is by automating customer service such as automated chatbots, which can be used to answer customer inquiries that fall within a predefined set of rules or responses. Furthermore, AI-driven algorithms can be used to streamline customer information and create data-driven customer profiles with insights about their preferences, behaviors, interests, and purchases. This allows businesses to effectively target potential customers, providing a more personalized experience in an increasingly competitive market.

AI technology can also help businesses streamline their workflows, which can lead to greater productivity and efficiency. AI can be used to automate tedious tasks, freeing up employees to focus on more complex tasks. AI-driven tools and applications can also help employees complete tasks faster, as they are trained to quickly and accurately understand the context of the query and provide the best solution. This leads to greater productivity and better employee performance.

AI can also automate mundane, repetitive tasks, which can include accounting, taxes, and payroll. AI-driven algorithms can be used to automatically calculate required payments to clients and vendors and can be integrated with existing systems to simplify the process of accounting and taxes. This helps businesses focus on more strategic tasks, as the burden of mundane tasks is removed.

The integration of AI into workflows also provides better insights and data analysis. AI-powered tools allow businesses to accurately identify trends in customer behavior, which makes it easier to anticipate customer needs and provide better customer service. Furthermore, AI-driven solutions can be used to track customer sentiment, which can be used to discover product gaps and areas of improvement.

AI has the potential to unlock powerful productivity gains. Automating mundane tasks and increasing the accuracy of data analysis leads to greater efficiency and faster problem-solving. AI goes beyond simple automation, by allowing businesses to access deeper insights into customer behavior. This can empower more effective decision-making, leading to greater success in the long run. Although AI still has considerable potential to unlock, it is already providing groundbreaking benefits to businesses today, and the future of AI holds much promise.

Chapter 29: "Lighten Your Load: Harnessing the Power of AI Automation to Streamline Routine Tasks and Enhance Workplace Productivity."

The importance of harnessing the power of AI automation to streamline routine tasks and enhance workplace productivity cannot be overstated. AI technology has made it possible to automate mundane, repetitive tasks, allowing workers to focus on more value-added tasks and projects. This not only increases productivity, but also help ease the strain on workers by lightening their workload.

AI automation can cover a wide range of industries and tasks. Automation tools can be used to automate customer service, marketing campaigns, data entry and analytic, and even more sensitive tasks such as reviewing contracts or analytics. By employing automated solutions, businesses can increase efficiency and standardize processes, increasing the speed and quality of work.

Using AI solutions to automate was previously done by offshoring tasks to other countries or hiring freelancers. By harnessing AI, outsourcing is no longer necessary, and companies can access advanced technology with minimal effort. Not only is cost savings achieved, but businesses can also trust the accuracy and security of the process. AI solutions provide access to machines learning capabilities and artificial intelligence, allowing it to quickly and accurately produce desirable results.

The ways businesses are adopting AI automation technology to streamline their processes continues to evolve. For example, companies are using AI bots to conduct interviews and commence new employees, enabling people to start working faster and more efficiently. AI is also being used to automate the handling of customer inquiries, meaning customers get faster response times and better service. In the manufacturing industry, AI-driven robots are reducing labor costs and increasing production efficiency, while in the finance industry, sophisticated AI algorithms are being used to accurately detect fraud and attempt to prevent money laundering.

The impact of automation on workplace productivity has been far-reaching, as employees no longer need to spend hours or days on mundane activities. Instead, they are free to focus on problem-solving, creative, and strategic activities. Employee satisfaction increases, and they become more motivated and productive, leading to further gains in efficiency. Moreover, automated processes often eliminate human errors, increasing the accuracy and quality of work.

Harnessing the power of AI for automated tasks can lead to significant cost savings. Apart from reducing the need for manual labor, AI-driven solutions can identify and exploit inefficiencies quicker, streamlining processes and improving the bottom line.

AI automation has revolutionized workplace productivity. By harnessing the power of AI automation in the workplace, businesses are increasing efficiency, cost savings, and productivity, with minimal effort. Automation can be used to streamline routine tasks, allowing employees to focus on more valuable activities, and providing higher quality of work. Moreover, AI offers enhanced safety through accurate and direction-free automated processes. By incorporating AI automation in your workplace, you can lighten your load and enjoy the benefits in no time.

Chapter 30: "Maximizing Efficiency Through AI Automation: Achieving Improved Productivity in the Workplace."

Artificial intelligence (AI) has quickly become one of the most talked about topics in the workplace, as organizations of all sizes are looking to adopt AI solutions for the purpose of improving efficiency and productivity. AI can be used to automate repetitive or time-consuming tasks that currently take away from time that could be dedicated to higher-value activities, and in doing so, it helps to reduce on the whole costs and free up resources for other priorities.

In order to get the most out of AI automation in the workplace, it is important to begin by identifying the tasks that could be automated and the goals that need to be achieved through automation. This could include automating mundane tasks such as data entry, customer service inquiries, or social media management, or it could be more complex tasks such as decision-making or analytics. The key is to select the right tasks and the right tools to make the automation process as efficient as possible.

Once the goals of the automation process have been identified, the next step is to develop a strategy and plan for implementing the automation. This should include items such as mapping out the data flows, determining the best AI model and algorithms to use, and designing the user interface so that it is easy to use and understand. It should also include setting up a system to track the progress and success of the AI automation so that it can be monitored and adjusted if necessary.

It is important to ensure that when AI automation is implemented in the workplace, it is done so in a way that avoids disruption to employees and their work. AI systems can be trained to help employees with tasks that they find tedious or difficult, and in many cases, the AI system can even make suggestions about how to improve the current process.

No matter what type of AI automation is implemented in the workplace, the goal is to free up time and resources so that employees can spend more time on higher-value activities. AI automation can be used to automate mundane tasks or more complex tasks that require decision-making, and when used correctly, it can help organizations achieve greater efficiency and better productivity in the workplace.

Don't miss out!

Visit the website below and you can sign up to receive emails whenever Adam Smith publishes a new book. There's no charge and no obligation.

https://books2read.com/r/B-A-OSAW-ESGLC

BOOKS 2 READ

Connecting independent readers to independent writers.

Also by Adam Smith

AI in K-12 Education

Intelligent Machines in the Classroom: Unlocking the Potential of AI in K12 Education
Exploring the Possibilities: A Guide to Artificial Intelligence in K-12 Education
Exploring the Possibilities: AI in K12 Education
Making Sense of AI in K12 Education: A Guide for Teachers, Administrators, and Parents
The Future of Learning: Artificial Intelligence in K12 Education
Towards an AI-Infused Revolution in K12 Education
Unleashing AI in the Classroom: Strategies for Implementing Intelligent Technologies in K-12 Education
Unleashing the Potential of Artificial Intelligence in K-12 Education: Reimagining How Learning Happens
AI-Powered Learning: Advancing K12 Education for the 21st Century

AI in the Workplace

The AI Edge: Unlocking Increased Productivity in Life and Work

Breaking Down Bad Habits

Breaking Down Bad Habits: How to Overcome Self-Defeating Behaviors and Achieve Success

Standalone

Brain Dead: When It Comes To Improving Mental Health, What The Hell Are We Waiting For?

40 Things Intelligent People Do Daily

The Beginner's Guide to Quantum Computing & Mechanics

Open Source AI

Watch for more at https://books2read.com/adamsmith.

About the Author

Adam Smith is a native North Texas Entrepreneur, AI educational expert, and educator who graduated from Embry Riddle University with a Bachelor of Science in Aerospace Studies. In 2007 he co-founded TeacherTube.com, an online education platform community that provides an educationally focused, safe venue for teachers, schools, and home learners. Under his leadership, in September of 2017, a publicly traded company, Salem Media Group, acquired TeacherTube.

After the acquisition, Adam continued his passion for technology and education by helping schools and start-ups to large corporations with digital consulting.

Read more at https://books2read.com/adamsmith.

www.ingramcontent.com/pod-product-compliance
Lightning Source LLC
LaVergne TN
LVHW090429210926
848480LV00002B/754